IMAGES OF ENGLAND

BEWDLEY

IMAGES OF ENGLAND

BEWDLEY

BEWDLEY HISTORICAL RESEARCH GROUP

TEMPUS

Frontispiece: Walking to Ribbesford church, the parish church for
Bewdley, down Ribbesford Avenue.

First published 2005

Tempus Publishing Limited
The Mill, Brimscombe Port,
Stroud, Gloucestershire, GL5 2QG
www.tempus-publishing.com

© Bewdley Historical Research Group, 2005

The right of Bewdley Historical Research Group to
be identified as the Authors of this work has been
asserted in accordance with the Copyrights,
Designs and Patents Act 1988.

British Library Cataloguing in Publication Data.
A catalogue record for this book is available from the British Library.

ISBN 0 7524 3513 2

Typesetting and origination by Tempus Publishing Limited.
Printed in Great Britain.

Contents

Acknowledgements

Bewdley Historical Research Group is grateful for all the help given to them in the production of this book. Many have loaned photographs and offered help with historical facts.

The Group would like to thank the following, without whom there would be no book: M. Colman, D. Faul, D. Flack, B. Gale, K. Hobson, T. Holloway, E. Hurst, Mrs P. Mills, I. Moone, Mrs J. Moseley, Mrs J. Pagett, C. Purcell, C. Quayle, R. Webb, National Monuments Record, Worcestershire County Museum, Wyre Forest District Council Museum Service (Bewdley Museum).

Introduction

Bewdley, situated on the River Severn, has over the centuries won the admiration of writers such as John Leland, (1539), William Camden, (*c.* 1600) and William Stukeley, (1712) and offers the present-day visitor riverside walks, interesting buildings, pleasant scenery and, a little way beyond the town, the Wyre Forest. The name Bewdley is in fact derived from the French *beau lieu* – a beautiful place. This name, however, is not recorded before 1275 but there is reason to believe that the name Wribbenhall formerly referred to what is now Bewdley.

Historically the manor belonged to the powerful Mortimer family, Lords of the Marches, who paid a yearly rent of twenty shillings to Worcester Priory for land at Wribbenhall but later paid this sum as rent for Bewdley, which suggests that the places were one and the same. Some of the Mortimers occasionally lived at Tickenhill, which was used as a dower house for the widow of the Lord.

The River Severn could for many centuries be described as the lifeblood of Bewdley as much of the prosperity of the town, especially during its Golden Age (1660-1760), derived from river trade. Records show that an amazing variety of goods were transported up and down the river; Bewdley men were trading on the Severn as early as 1308. In 1411 they were accused by Gloucester and Bristol traders of not allowing them to pass upriver unless they agreed to hire 'great boats called trows' owned by the Bewdley men for the carriage of their goods. In 1504 several Bewdley men were involved in a Star Chamber case in which they complained that they were set upon with stones and arrows if they attempted to sail past the quays at Worcester.

The Minister's Accounts of 1472 mention High Street–as Over or Upper Street,– Wyre Hill, Welch Gate, Lax Lane and Dog Lane, but Load Street and Severn Side did not appear to exist at that time. Load Street was developed before 1540, as Leland wrote

at the rising of the sun from the East the whole town glittereth (being of all new building) as it were of gold. There be but three Streets memorable in the Towne, one from

7

the North to South all along Severn Bank. The second is the Market place, a fair large thinge and well builded. The third runneth from North to South on the Hill side, as the first doth in the Valley of Severne.

Bewdley remained a vibrant inland port until the late eighteenth century. With the development of industry in the surrounding West Midland area, as well as in Gloucester and Bristol, more movement of cargoes was necessary. Among the proposals put forward for canal schemes in 1766 was one by James Brindley. The terrain around Bewdley, however, proved to be problematic and would have required a long tunnel through Summer House Hill to the Stour Valley. Brindley therefore diverted his canal to Stourport.

Bewdley's economy changed as merchants moved to Stourport, but it was at this time that wealthy families built many of the large houses and the frontages of shops and houses were refaced in accordance with prevailing fashion. The appearance of the town changed considerably and has remained much the same ever since.

Bewdley Historical Research Group

The Group started in 1980 when a number of individuals who were interested in the history of Bewdley met under the umbrella of Birmingham University ExtraMural Department. Initially the members began tracing the history of one street using the Bewdley Manor Court Rolls which began in 1655. These were made available by the Lord of the Manor, a member of the Group. From this it progressed to other streets within the Conservation Area of Bewdley. To add interest the probates for Bewdley, held at Hereford Record Office, were transcribed and indexed. It soon became obvious that the research could not be limited to Bewdley but must also cover Ribbesford (the original parish), Dowles and Wribbenhall.

The aim of the Group has always been to make the information gathered available to all, and to this end a number of books have been published. Initially the period 1660–1760, Bewdley's Golden Age, was the centre of research but as the years have passed a much wider period has been studied. Two volumes of *Bewdley in its Golden Age* have been printed (Volume One is now out of print) and two books of photographs have previously been published but are both now out of print.

As a summer activity the Group has recorded all the stones in the local churchyards and made them available to the Birmingham and Midland Society for Genealogy and Heraldry who transferred them to fiche for general use.

To meet the interest of people in the history of their homes and tracing their family history, Group members have, for some years, staffed a Local History Room within Bewdley Museum on one morning a week. During the museum's closed winter season appointments are necessary but generally people can just 'drop in'.

Unfortunately membership numbers of the Group have to be restricted due to the constraints of the meeting venue. However, there is still much to be discovered and published by a group of enthusiastic amateurs.

one

The River

An early fording place on the river was at Lax Lane and the first mention of a ferry was in 1336. By 1381 it was making £2 annual profit, which had doubled by 1424. The Bishop of Worcester granted indulgences to all who contributed towards the cost of the bridge in 1447. That bridge was destroyed in the Wars of the Roses and in 1483 Richard III gave 200 marks for the erection of a stone bridge. It was a five-arched bridge with a wooden gatehouse over the third pillar on the Bewdley side and a timber chapel at the west end. Part of the bridge was swept away in 1574 and the remainder was damaged in the Civil Wars. Accounts show that snow and ice necessitated many repairs during its lifetime. Eventually the 'Great Flood' of 1795 caused such extensive damage that it had to be replaced. An Act was passed for a new bridge with a toll-house to be built. Thomas Telford was engaged to design the bridge, which was to be of stone. It was started and completed in 1798, the old bridge being repaired sufficiently for temporary use. Regrettably the toll-house was demolished in 1960.

Severn Side North, or Coal's Quay as it was known, would have been a hive of activity in the seventeenth and eighteenth centuries when Bewdley was an important inland port. This late nineteenth-century photograph shows just one barge moored against a tumbledown quay wall. In the 1890s the quay wall was rebuilt. Note the high entrances to the properties, to prevent flooding.

Bewdley Rowing Club started in around 1845 and its headquarters from the early 1880s until after the second World War was a raft moored below the bridge on the east bank of the river. In 1949 a wooden clubhouse and a Nissen hut boathouse were erected further upriver near the present site of the club. The present boathouse was built in 1961.

After the decline of Bewdley as an inland port, the river alongside Severn Side North (or Coal's Quay) was used for mooring pleasure boats and hotel landing stages. This postcard of 1912 shows the George Hotel landing stage to the right of the fisherman. Dowles railway bridge can be seen in the distance.

Severn Side South, before 1921. A pile of timber lies where the bandstand was built in 1921. Built on the site of Jonathan Skey's engine house and warehouse, the bank on the right began in 1832 as Bewdley Bank run by Messrs Nichols, Nichols and Crane. It later became a branch of the Birmingham and Midland Bank with Mr Alfred Clinch as manager. When the bank closed and moved to Load Street in 1967, Mr Bert Perrin was the manager.

The bandstand was erected in 1921 as a result of funds raised by Bewdley and Wribbenhall Brass Band Society. When Mr Mark Round opened the Garden Cinema in 1921 he gave the proceeds of the first performance to the bandstand fund. With the demise of the band, it was not used for many years and Bewdley Borough Council removed the roof in 1965. The remainder was removed to make way for flood defences.

The river was also home to the Floating Swimming Baths which were opened in 1884. They were moored on the east bank of the river – sometimes north of the bridge but sometimes on the south side. Of German design, fifty feet long and twenty feet wide, they could accommodate fifty people at a time. There was an exit into the river to allow access for swimming.

The Bewdley Floating Swimming Baths Company was formed on 23 July 1883 with a capital of £500 in £1 shares. It had nineteen subscribers. The Company Directors were Lloyd Davies, Reverend J.R. Burton, C.H. Westley, L.A. Gabb and T.D. Potter. At a meeting of shareholders in February 1885 Mr Westley commented on the very successful results with 'a great number of persons learning to swim, which was sufficient reward to the Directors for their efforts'.

When the river is high, as can be seen in this 1960s photograph, the properties in Lax Lane, including the old National School seen here on the right, get flooded. However, the current defence work aims to prevent future floods. The name 'Lax' comes from a Scandinavian word for salmon. A river crossing or lode was established at the bottom of the lane to link up with Whispering (Westbourne) Street in Wribbenhall.

Load Street flooding in 1947. This is the highest flood in living memory although several others have come close to it. As the water rose, duckboards were erected for people to walk onto the bridge. A similar arrangement was erected on the Wribbenhall side of the bridge and down Pewterers' Alley to help people avoid Beales Corner that also flooded badly.

In December 1890 the river froze over in Bewdley. The coldest night of the year was Sunday 28 December. Many people took advantage of the opportunity to skate. The ice was good between Dowles Railway Bridge and the Severn Bridge but south of this, down to Ribbesford, the ice was dangerously thin. Although thousands skated almost daily over several weeks not a single accident of a serious nature occurred from the ice giving way. When the ice began to thaw it caused fear that the bridge might be washed away due to the pressure upon the pillars. The loss of river craft was considerable and amongst the boats damaged was the Floating Swimming Baths. They were later recovered and repaired. Many people's livelihoods were threatened and the Blackford Coal, Blanket and Clothing Fund was of considerable help to poor families.

Severe weather conditions preceding the severe flooding of the winter 1946/47. Charles Brown, former manager of the tannery on Severn Side South, is standing on the iced-over river at Blackstone.

Left: In the early 1950s the parapet of Telford's Bridge was removed, as well as some of the poor stone on the bridge itself. A new parapet was erected.

Below: The railway inspectors' train, looking rather like a toy train on a Meccano bridge, crossing Dowles railway bridge over the River Severn on 9 August 1865, shortly before the opening of the Tenbury and Bewdley Railway. The contractor, Thomas Brassey, is thought to have used the barge on the right. The bridge was demolished in 1964 and only the piers remain.

two

Street Scenes
and Traders

James Ward's basket–makers shop at No. 4 Severn Side South. He had previously traded from 1884 to 1896 at No. 75 Load Street.

A succession of printers occupied No. 11 Load Street over the years. A printing business was established by 1754 but there is no further detail of the proprietor. In 1855 Thomas Edward Dalley was running the business and by 1904 it had passed to Ernest P. Shepherd who ran it as a printer's and stationer's. Around 1912 Shepherd took on H.G. Perkins to run the printing side of the business. By 1923 Shepherd had retired and T.F.W. Harris was trading as the printer and stationer. The Dalley family had returned to the business again by 1953. It is now Vantage Chemist's.

Left: The Sisters' Shop in 1948. It was run by the Mapp sisters, Adelaide Ellen and Clarice May, and sold confectionery, tobacco and cigarettes, newspapers and stationery. They also sold knitting wools. The premises are now used as a hairdresser's – The Cutting Room'

Below: An 1860s photograph of Thomas Pountney's game-dealing shop on the corner of Load Street and Park Lane. Pountney was also a hatter, a trade which many years previously had been an important part of Bewdley's economy. This building had replaced an earlier property used as a shop by the Pountney family. The replacement shop was demolished in the 1960s as part of the road-widening scheme.

A well-stocked greengrocer's at No. 41 Load Street, *c.* 1900. Richard Bowdler, fishmonger and fruiterer, followed his father William into the trade. William's shop was in Park Butts, Kidderminster. Richard's brother Frederick had taken over the business by 1912 and the shop continued as a greengrocer's and fishmonger's for many years. Until recently the premises traded as The Emporium, a general antique and bric-a-brac shop.

The India and China Tea Co. at No. 47 Load Street was owned by Joseph Burton & Sons and was managed in 1916 by William James, who can be seen here on the extreme left with his son John (Jack) by his side. William's wife Molly is in the shop doorway with Irene in the pram. William later had his own grocery shop at No. 45 Load Street and this was carried on by Jack after his death.

A busy day in Bewdley, *c.* 1910. Note the little boy standing by a lamp-post near the west end of St Anne's church – not possible with today's traffic.

Burton's grocery shop in 1930. On the left in the doorway is Edgar George Holloway, who was the manager. On his left is his assistant Billie Perkins. The shop had been a grocer's for many years with Edward Balley taking over from John Anderson in 1916. Later, in the 1920s, Thomas Sutcliffe traded from there. Burton's took over in around 1929 and continued there into the 1960s.

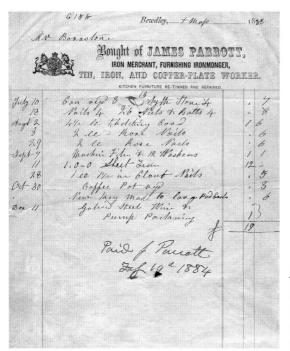

James Parrott, born in Leeds, in around 1826, first traded in Bewdley in 1861 when he was employing one man and a boy in his shop. He had moved from the shop at No. 58 Load Street to No. 28 Load Street by 1891.

Edwin Dudfield took over the ironmonger's shop at No. 58 Load Street from James Parrott in 1891. The premises were considered unsafe when Spar, the present occupiers, took over and the façade was rebuilt.

Above: When Edwin Dudfield died in 1902 Harry Joseph Exley took over the ironmongery business at No. 58 Load Street (the '8' is hidden behind a roll of netting). Exley ran a small brass foundry at the rear. He later moved across the road to No. 17 and ran a retail shop in front of a much larger brass foundry (now part of Bewdley Museum).

Left: Les Key behind the counter in Wrenson's grocery shop, in around 1960, before moving to his own shop at No. 54 (now The Bear Pit).

Left: J.H. Parkes opened Bewdley Dining Rooms near the bridge in the 1920s. The dining rooms would probably have been very well used by the visitors to the town from Birmingham and the Black Country.

Below: This is the shop now trading as Teddy Gray's at No. 1 Load Street. Miss Annie Hinton is in the doorway of the shop that at this time, around 1910, was owned by Miss Susan Field. In the 1940s a Mrs Wilcox ran the shop as a confectioner's.

The Borough Stores on the corner of Load Street and High Street had been a grocery business since 1700 when John Prattinton, grocer, owned it. It passed through several generations of the Prattinton family but towards the end of the eighteenth century it came into the hands of Benjamin Owens, grocer. He was succeeded by his son Thomas in 1840. Owens served the people of Bewdley and the surrounding district for many years for both wholesale and retail goods. A very wide range of goods, including some luxury items, was available. In 1904 the premises were sold to Henry Hillier when the name Borough Stores came into use. For some years Hillier ran the business in partnership with Arthur Gristwood, grocer. By 1932 Evans Brothers were managing the shop for Gristwood and they eventually bought it.

The north end of High Street, showing No. 68, the handsome seventeenth-century building commonly known as the Bailiff's House. It was owned by Thomas Boylston, a prominent bailiff in the early seventeenth century, his initials 'T.B.' and the date '1610' being carved over the door. At the end of the nineteenth century, until around 1901, No. 67 next door was used by Samuel Tudge as his blacksmith's shop.

Above: Frank Heydon started his bakery business in around 1908 and his wife Emily is seen here with Lillian Dorrell and Mabel Johnson. After Heydon the business was run by J.W. Wadeley until 1940 when A.H. Gillam took over. The shop remained a bakery business right up until the 1980s.

Left: George Cross, who is seen here collecting a box of fish from Bewdley railway station, ran a fried fish business at No. 14 Welch Gate from around 1940.

The Wagon and Horses in Welch Gate in around 1896 when Charles Smith was the licensee. By 1904 he had moved next door to the Anchor Inn.

Alfred Richard Maunder and his wife Margaret ran the Packhorse Inn from around 1895 until 1928. Alfred was a local councillor for many years and was mayor in 1900. Margaret died in 1905. The inn was a regular meeting place for the Bewdley Working Men's Sick and Dividend Society until 1895. The inn also served as the headquarters for the Bewdley and District Terrier Club and the Bewdley Homing Society. It remained licensed premises until 1961.

Above and below: Alfred Maunder ran a successful inn and posting establishment and operated an omnibus between Bewdley and Kidderminster. He also hired out brakes for weddings and civic occasions.

Before the building of Bewdley bypass the main road from the town towards the west passed through Welch Gate, an area of terraced housing bordering a narrow road across which a toll-gate was erected. There were a number of inns to cater for the needs of the travellers entering or leaving the town. These old houses were often dilapidated; sanitary arrangements were basic and water had to be drawn from wells even until the beginning of the twentieth century. They were occupied in the main by labourers and craftsmen such as basket-makers and besom-makers, many of whom worked in the forest.

Welch Gate/Winbrook is the site for this posed photograph, taken during a celebration – possibly Queen Victoria's Diamond Jubilee. The ladies and children are dressed in their finery. The large building in the background is No. 17 Welch Gate – the Star and Garter inn.

Sandy Bank at one time had a row of beautiful medieval timber-framed houses but in the early 1970s they were demolished to make way for the gardens of the modern bungalows in Orchard Rise, off Park Lane.

This oil painting shows the inn, The Old Town Hall, on Wyre Hill on the left. Merricks Lane is on the right, just beyond the hay wagon.

The Midland Bank, which had absorbed the Bewdley Bank, was on Severn Side South in the 1960s when this interior shot was taken. Mr John Tomes is serving Miss Humpherson. It was, more recently, used as a craft shop and studio by a local artist.

By the 200th anniversary of the bank in 1982, Mr Jeff Gait was the manager. He is displaying examples of early Bewdley £5 bank notes. The bank had moved from Severn Side South to Load Street in 1967.

Above: There are indications that Wribbenhall House was originally a medieval dwelling which was given a facelift in the eighteenth century to make it more fashionable. For some time it was the Black Boy and Raven inn, but in 1807 it was sold to William Cartwright and used as a private house. It remained in the Cartwright family until 1879 when it was sold to George Crane. After his death it was rented out, until finally it was bought by the County Council for £1,250 in 1933 and pulled down for road widening. The present police station occupies part of the former site.

Left: The interior of Wribbenhall post office, Kidderminster Road, in the 1970s with Postmaster Mr Joe Garbett.

In the 1920s Thomas Jenks opened the Central Garage in Wribbenhall (the site of the present Texaco petrol station). It was later run for many years by the Hoare family.

Bewdley Service Station, Kidderminster Road, on a day in the 1970s when petrol had one shilling off every gallon. The service station no longer exists – the site is to be redeveloped. In the background can be seen Storrage House, with its main façade at right angles to the road. At one time the vicarage for Wribbenhall, it is now used for offices.

This row of cottages at Catchem's End, Wribbenhall became known as Letterbox Row and stood next to the present fish and chip shop. The cottages were demolished in the 1960s.

Most of these people can be identified. The photograph was taken in 1916 at the junction of Habberley Road and Kidderminster Road. The man with the child is Mr Cope, who lived across the road in Letterbox Row, and next to him is Mr R. Jackson, the headmaster of Lax Lane School. The lady with the sunshade is Mrs Kirkham, who lived at Lansdown, a house opposite on the Kidderminster Road. Mr Jorden of Bank Cottage is crossing the road and Mr Jones watches from his garden.

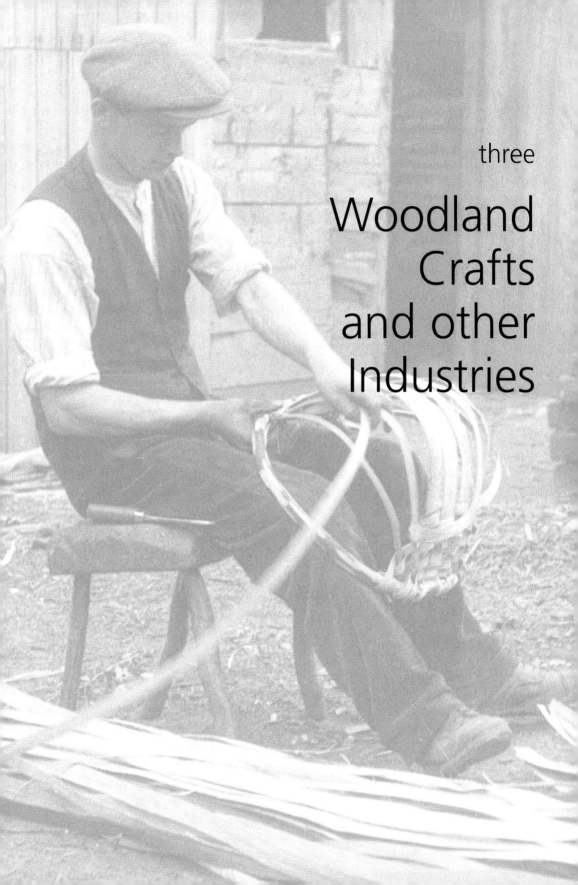

three

Woodland Crafts and other Industries

Joseph Oakes was a local timber merchant and this photograph shows one of his wagons crossing Dowles Brook in 1917.

A group of forestry workers in Wyre Forest. They seem to be mostly woodcutters as they have axes with them but one or two, such as the man on the extreme right, have barking irons in their hands.

George Carter and his family – perhaps his sons and grandsons – have felled a mature oak tree and are tidying it up before it is sent to the saw yard.

The strength of shire horses was needed to pull laden wagons of timber and here a team extracts timber from Ribbesford Woods. This load may have been going to the sawmill of T.H. Williams in Severn Side South. Later, tractors replaced the horses and felled timber would be loaded onto the bogie or trailer. Timber merchants would work closely with the woodmen and fellers.

Above: Timber is a multi-purpose material and here men are sawing pit props in Wyre Forest. The many mines in the area surrounding Bewdley would need plentiful supplies.

Left: Timber was cut into planks with a pit saw, prior to mechanical saws being used. The top sawyer had the superior job, the unfortunate bottom sawyer being perpetually showered with sawdust. This is where the expression 'topdog' and 'underdog' came from.

Above and below: Charcoal burning was rough and demanding and to some extent dependent on the weather. Once the clamp was lit it had to be watched continuously night and day until the process, which usually took eight to ten days, was completed. The men preferred to work in pairs so that one could always be present and awake. For shelter, the woodcolliers, blackened by smoke, built huts of branches covered by a tarpaulin or mud. They ate bread, cheese, bacon and perhaps the occasional rabbit, and drank ale, tea or cider.

Above and below: Before the process could begin, a floor about fifteen feet in diameter had to be levelled and a six-foot pole placed in the centre. The wood for burning had to be purchased by the men or by a Master Woodcollier who employed them. Pieces of wood, each three feet long, were wheeled from the coppice to the site on barrows and these had to be placed sloping towards the centre pole. Other lengths of wood were arranged so that the end product was a dome-shaped construction of some six feet high and fifteen feet in diameter. The whole was then draught proofed with turf or damp earth and the centre pole removed, leaving a chimney.

Once the clamp was draught proofed, hot charcoal and kindling would be dropped through the central hole and the chimney blocked to exclude air. It was then left to burn slowly for several days. The charcoal burner would have to cover places where the fire broke through by shovelling on soil and patting it down. Once the burning was completed, the charcoal was allowed to cool. To hasten the cooling process, the clamp was sometimes doused with water before the charcoal was shovelled into sacks for sale. The next clamp would then be prepared in this continuous operation.

In the 1940s a new style of production was introduced using metal retorts. This eased the work of the charcoal burners considerably.

In the 1980s Bewdley Museum carried out several reconstruction burns in Wyre Forest and staff and volunteers worked together. A retired charcoal burner, Joe Nevey, was on hand to advise. Several people are sorting and moving wood. From left to right: Mike ?, Dave Darby, Charlie Fogg, Peter Hobson and Andy Holding.

Bark-peeling was an important part of the work in the forest as it produced a basic material for the local tanneries to use in the processing of hides. The peeling was mainly done by women and children as shown in this 1908 photograph.

This group of bark-peelers in Wyre Forest shows that men did do some bark-peeling. Note the impractical clothing, especially the hat worn by the woman standing third from right, perhaps for the occasion of the photograph.

Another group of bark-peelers, this time in the 1930s. Note the obviously cut-down adult coat that the girl is wearing. The bark was removed using a barking iron, a small slightly dished piece of metal on a short handle.

The oak bark, which needed to be dried for use in the tanneries, is laid out on a rack in Ribbesford Woods.

Taken in 1926, this photograph shows dried oak bark being unloaded at one of the many tanneries in Severn Side South. Note the spelk baskets used for carrying the smaller pieces up the ladders into storage rooms. The bark would be kept for about six months and then ground up before being added to water in a pit to provide liquor for hides to be soaked in. Looking on is the postman, Billy Griffiths.

Left: Besom-making was another of the crafts to use forest supplies. Here, in the 1930s, birch twigs are being collected for use in making the brushes.

Below: Besom-making in the yard of No. 15 Wyre Hill, the home of Christopher Birch and his family. He also worked with the Bishop family. Birch twigs were tied together with a strip of oak or willow and then a hazelwood handle was inserted to make a very versatile brush.

Left: Forest workers were often multi-skilled. Here birch twigs are being stripped to make whisks, small brooms used mainly in the carpet industry to remove flights of fluff from the woven carpet. A pile of oak scuttles (baskets) suggests that this man makes several different products.

Below: Christopher Birch in his yard on Wyre Hill in the 1950s making oak scuttles. The steaming bosch, or boiler, which provided hot water to soak the oak to make it more pliable, can be seen in the background.

Spelk-basket-making on Wyre Hill during the mid-twentieth century. From left to right: Christopher Birch, Mr Bishop and Benjamin Brown.

ALL IN WANT OF A **GOOD OAK SCUTTLE**

SHOULD APPLY TO

BEN. BROWN

3, LAX LANE, BEWDLEY.

The Master of all Masters!

The only Man in the Trade that has ever made a Four Peck SQUARE BASKET in Seventeen Minutes!

Timed by Mr. T. Dalloway; witnessed by Messrs. B. Dalloway, W. Bishop, sen., and half-a-dozen others.

ORDERS PROMPTLY ATTENDED TO. PRICES MODERATE.

Trade card of Benjamin Brown, advertising his skill at making a large basket.

Lowe's ropeworks, established in 1801, lay at right angles to the later Severn Valley Railway. The viaduct carried the rails over Kidderminster Road. The site has now been developed for residential housing. Ropewalk Cottage survives.

George Taylor twisting raw fibre, probably flax, into strands from which the final rope could be twisted using the number of strands required for a finished rope of a particular strength.

Some of the machinery needed for rope-making was very simple, as can be seen here. William Bond, who left school at fourteen years of age to take his first job at Lowe's ropeworks in 1916, is standing on the sledge. This moved up as the twisting together of the strands shortened the rope. Stones were added or removed depending on the weight of the rope.

This posed photograph is thought to be at the Northwood (Rag) Lane rope-making site. The identity of only one man is known – George Taylor, on the extreme right. The date of closure of this site is not known but Lowe's, on Kidderminster Road, made its last rope in 1972.

G. J. HUMPHERSON & SONS

(Late G. J. & J. Humpherson,)

THE HORN WORKS BEWDLEY

ESTBBLISH·D, 1749.

Manufacturers of Foresters', Holster, Drenching and Powder Horns and Flasks,

---

PORTABLE AND DRINKING HORNS.

All kinds of Combs, Shoe Lifts, Scoops, and Spoons, Salt Cellars, Pepper and Tobacco Boxes, Lanthorn Leaves, &c., &c.

[P.T.O.]

Above and below: A Humpherson trade card which lists a very wide range of horn products made by the firm.

G. J. HUMPHERSON & SONS

(Late G. J. & J. Humpherson),

THE HORN WORKS, BEWDLEY

(ESTABLISHED 1749.

EVERY DESCRIPTION OF HORN WORK SUITABLY MOUNTED IN BRASS, GERMAN SILVER, STERLING SILVER & GOLD.

WORK EXECUTED UPON THE PREMISES.

Secretaries of Foresters and Shepherds' Socities allowed a Liberal Commission.

Old Foresters' Horns repaired and remounted at Moderate Prices.

[P.T.O.]

Alfred Humpherson, probably seated second from left, and his men who worked in the horn manufactory in High Street. In 1839 James Humpherson, Alfred's grandfather, took out a lease from the Borough of Bewdley for the former poorhouse. The lease was to run for fourteen years at £20 per year. This building was used by the same family as a horn manufactory for many years until the early twentieth century.

The snuff mill in The Park behind Tickenhill was in use from the early nineteenth century through into the twentieth. The Humpherson family bought it from James Holder in 1867 and adapted the machinery to cut the teeth of horn combs.

Left: James 'Snuffy' Holder ran a snuff-making business in the snuff mill in The Park for many years. He was still running it in 1861 at the age of eighty-six. He died in 1867.

Below: An important business within Bewdley during the twentieth century was that of Herbert C. Styles, corn and seed merchant. In 1926 Styles had a warehouse in Station Yard but in 1927 he bought Severn House in Stourport Road and this eventually became the offices for the business. The house can be seen on the left behind the mill. Another division of the business was across the road near Victoria House. Both sites have now been developed and are private homes.

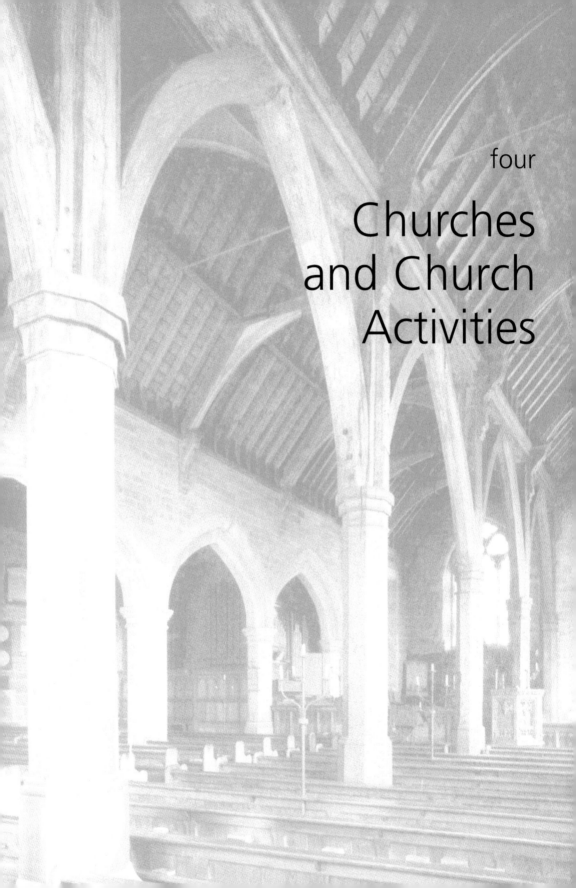

four

Churches and Church Activities

Above: The exterior of St Leonard's church at Ribbesford. It was conveniently situated for the gentry at Ribbesford House and is still the parish church for Bewdley.

Left: The oldest parts of the church date from 1100. It was enlarged later in the twelfth century and again in the fifteenth century. The south arcade is of timber, mainly Perpendicular work. It is formed by four rough-hewn octagonal posts with capitals to match, from which curved timbers meet to form pointed arches. The north arcade is of stone. The church underwent a major restoration in 1878 at a cost of £4,000 and examples of fresco painting were uncovered. Amongst the dedications on the windows is one over the west door to Hannah Macdonald, the grandmother of both Stanley Baldwin, the prime minister, and Rudyard Kipling, the writer. The window was made by William Morris from a design by Burne-Jones, the son-in-law of Hannah Macdonald.

St Anne's church, set in the centre of Load Street, replaced a Chapel of Ease made of timber. Originally dedicated to St Andrew it had three chantries – St Mary, St Anne and the Holy Trinity. In 1695 a stone tower was added, however in 1745 the chapel and tower were demolished and new ones built. The new tower was built mainly at the expense of the Rector of Ribbesford, Reverend Thomas Knight. Officially opened on Lady Day 1745 and dedicated to St Anne, its bells were recast in 1780. In 1928 the tower was restored under the direction of Giles Gilbert Scott.

The interior of St Anne's church showing the balcony, part of which was subsequently removed, and the organ which is now in the remaining part of the balcony.

Christ Church was built in 1701 but was demolished in 1880 after All Saints' church had been built. In 1841 Wribbenhall had become an independent chapelry and had its own registers from that time. Up to then all entries for baptisms, marriages and burials were made in the registers of St Mary's, Kidderminster.

This Garden of Rest was the site of Christ Church. The lych gate was designed by Miss Fanny Hartland and given by Reverend Charles Warner in around 1850 in memory of his friend Reverend William Hallen, who was in charge of the parish from 1833-1849. The former National School (Church of England), built in 1850, can be seen behind the lych gate.

All Saints' church was built in 1878 on land given by Walter Chamberlain Hemming of Spring Grove. The land had been consecrated for burial purposes since 1866. Walter Hemming died in 1873 but his widow, Fanny, laid the foundation stone. The design was entrusted to Mr (later Sir) Arthur Blomfield who chose an early nineteenth-century style built of Alveley stone. The church became part of a group comprising Wribbenhall, Bewdley, Far Forest, Rock and Heightington in 1976.

All Saints' church boys' choir is seen here on their way to sing in Worcester in 1902.

Above: St Andrew's church, Dowles, was built in 1789 to replace an earlier building. The semi-circular apse was added in 1882 together with new windows. By around 1931 the church had fallen into disuse and the ecclesiastical parish was united with Bewdley. The Church Commissioners gave permission to demolish the building and in March 1956 this was done. The burial ground and ruins of the Parish Room can still be found just below the confluence of the Dowles Brook.

Left: The present Roman Catholic church of the Holy Family was built as a Presbyterian Chapel in around 1778, during the ministry of John Jones, on the site of an earlier church. It became a Unitarian Meeting House but the congregation dwindled and it closed in 1894. It was leased to the Baptists for a short while but then became a workshop and storage depot of a local builder. In 1951 the building became available for sale and was purchased for the Archdiocese as a Chapel of Ease. Restoration was completed and the church was officially opened in 1953.

The interior of the Roman Catholic church when it was used as a builder's store.

Bewdley's Nonconformist churches

The turmoil of the Reformation is hinted at in the Bridge and Chapel Wardens' Accounts for Bewdley: the town had two sets of burgesses trying to take power because of their differing beliefs. The establishment of the various denominations in Bewdley reflects the countrywide changes in religious belief. The Baptist breakaway came after the debate over infant baptism between Richard Baxter, curate at Kidderminster, and John Tombes who was chaplain of St Anne's Chapel, on New Year's Day 1650. Tombes, as a perpetual curate in the Chapel of Ease, was not obliged to baptise infants. After the day-long debate Baxter was satisfied that he had won, but Tombes had a group of eighteen supporters who formed a Baptist meeting. He was its first minister. By the end of the seventeenth century the Baptist cause in Bewdley appears to have been firmly established although its precise strength is difficult to assess. John Eckles, aged sixteen, had succeeded Tombes but he then moved to the Bromsgrove church.

The Quakers established themselves in 1691 at the end of Lower Park, off High Street on the King's Stable land. The original Presbyterian Meeting House was erected by Joseph Tyndall in 1696 and its first resident minister was Henry Oasland, who had been minister at St Anne's church until his secession in 1662. This became the Unitarian Meeting House when it was rebuilt in 1778 during the ministry of John Jones.

It was another century before the Methodist church was built, in around 1795, following several visits of John Wesley to the town, when he preached on the 'corner of the street'. The Methodists had been active for some years before, as *Berrow's Journal* records in August 1780 that at the assizes 'John Green and two others, were tried for riotously assaulting an assembly of Methodists at Wribbenhall. Green was fined £50 and ordered to lie in gaol until the money be paid. The others, through the clemency of the prosecutors, were set at liberty.'

The buildings still represent those divisions, though the Presbyterian Chapel in High Street has been a Catholic Chapel of Ease since 1953.

Above: Bewdley Quaker Meeting House, built in 1691, is tucked away behind other buildings on the edge of the town at the end of Lower Park. The Meeting House has been in constant use, albeit with fluctuating numbers, ever since. Numbers went down to just a handful of people but the Meeting was saved by the arrival of the Sturge and Tangye families. Charles Sturge was described as 'the mainstay of the Meeting' even though he did not minister. This title was given to him by Alice Tangye, later Parker, who would later take over that role herself. She kept the Meeting going through the darkest years, when membership was at its lowest ebb, until 1960 when she died. Most of the founder members of the Meeting were buried in the grounds of the Meeting House, as were several other local Quakers. The most prominent of these was Mary Darby, wife of Abraham Darby I, of Coalbrookdale. Alice Parker was also buried there.

Left: The exterior of the Methodist church has remained almost unchanged from the 1950s, when this photograph was taken, until the present day.

The Methodist church was renovated in 1956 and this photograph, taken in May of that year, shows the interior when the reopening and rededication service was taking place. The stained glass windows in the background commemorate Mr Thomas Owen's period of office as Mayor of Bewdley in 1902. Some time later the seats to the left were removed to make way for the grand piano presented to the church in memory of the organist Cliff Jones.

Sunday school anniversaries were popular up to the 1970s and this one is at the Methodist church in around 1960. From left to right, back row: Graham Bickley, Marilyn Bridgman, Mervyn Cross, Pat Dalloway. Middle row: Harold Dalloway, Paul Chambers, Fred Crowther, Mabel Crowther, Desiree Birch. Front row: Neil Sollom, David Finch, Alan Chambers, Stuart McKay, Linda Willis and Kathleen Lambert. The ladies in the choir are Betty Davies, Joyce Purcell and Lillian Bridgman.

This 1925 frontage to Bewdley Baptist church was radically changed in around 1926 when some Sunday school rooms were built. The interior was modernised in 1994 to give a comfortable meeting place and the sanctuary is now used for community events, such as a venue for Bewdley Festival, as well as the regular church meetings each week.

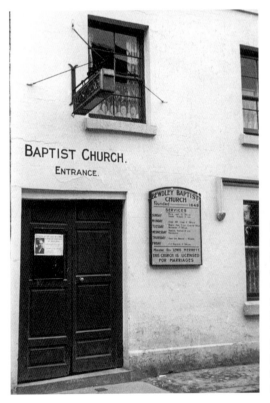

Bewdley Baptist church frontage, c. 1950. The eighteenth-century church is hidden behind these double doors, as Nonconformist churches could not be visible from the street. A church was first built on this site in the seventeenth century. Reverend Lewis Mwrrett was the Minister from February 1949 until December 1952. The property is now the church office. In the past it provided accommodation for the Minister or the caretaker. The poster on the door publicised the visit of an American evangelist, Reverend Roland Brown.

Sunday school prizegiving at Bewdley Baptist church in the 1960s.

The Wayfarers Youth Club was an important part of the Baptist church. It was run by Mr Stephen Quayle and his sister Miss Kathleen Quayle from the 1940s to the 1960s. The Tramps Supper seen here was an annual event and those in costume were expected to walk to the event so that the public could see them. Stephen Quayle also did this to set an example. From left to right, back row: Stephen Quayle, Bob Simmonds, Mike Martin, Dave Dalloway, Barry Key, Les Key. The names of those in the front row are not known.

In the 1950s Miss Gladys Aylward, a missionary from China, made a visit to Bewdley and a meeting was held at the Baptist church. From left to right: Mavis Breakwell, Miss Kathleen Quayle, Gladys Aylward, Ann Cooper. A biography of her life, *The Small Woman*, was written and the film *The Inn of the Sixth Happiness* was based on it.

St George's Hall, to the rear of the George Hotel, was originally built in Victorian times as an Assembly Room. It was bought by Bewdley Christian Community Hall, a charity, in 1965 and has been used ever since for community events. This Hunger Lunch of 1969 was to raise funds for missionary work. From left to right: Mrs Harward, Mrs 'Topsy' Beves and Reverend Gaston Harward, Rector of Ribbesford with Bewdley.

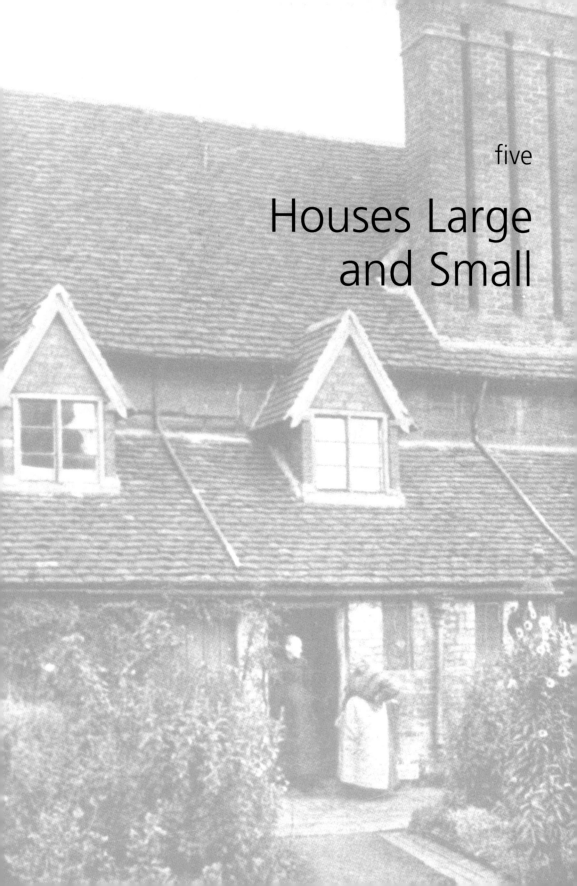

five

Houses Large and Small

· Old Tickenhill Palace ·

Tickenhill in 1712, as drawn by Dr Stukeley, compared with the same house today. In 1539 when John Leland visited Bewdley he wrote, 'There is a fayre Mannour place by West of the Towne standing in a goodly Park well wooded, on the very Knappe of an hill that the Town standeth on. This place is called Tickenhill'. This manor house had belonged to the powerful Mortimer family and may have been used as a dower house. It later passed to the Crown, was extended by Edward IV and rebuilt by Henry VII as a residence for Prince Arthur. It was here that the prince was married by proxy to Catherine of Aragon and here too that his body rested on its last journey to Worcester, where he is buried. In its heyday there was a park belonging to the manor house enclosing the grounds of Tickenhill, Kateshill and Winterdyne, with hunting to be had in the surrounding forest. The royal palace was built largely of timber and had a great court and garden with many outbuildings. In between occupation the building was often allowed to fall into disrepair and set in order to accommodate visiting royalty when required. One such renovation was made when it was intended that Mary, the daughter of Henry VIII, would live there but it is not clear whether she did in fact take up residence. When the important Council of the Marches met in Bewdley during the summer months, its president would reside in the palace. In 1641 King Charles I spent three nights there and during the Civil War, when a Royalist force had its quarters in the building, one wing was bombarded and damaged. The palace eventually passed into private hands and in around 1738 had its frontage rebuilt to give the appearance it has today.

Alice Tangye, seated on the right on the bench, as a young girl at Tickenhill, in around 1910. Alice, who was the daughter of Joseph Tangye, an engineer, is seen here with her brothers and sister. During her marriage to James Frederick Parker she became a notable local historian and wrote many books and papers.

J.F. (James Frederick) Parker and his wife Alice lived at Tickenhill in the mid-twentieth century. Over many years they built up a large collection of antiques and collectables and eventually opened several rooms at Tickenhill as a museum. When James died most of his collection was given to the county, some of which can still be seen at the County Museum in Hartlebury. The BBC used Tickenhill for several radio programmes and here James Parker is with Glyn Daniel of the *Animal, Vegetable, Mineral* programme in the 1950s.

Ribbesford House stands on the site of a house occupied by the De Ribbesfords in the time of Henry II. The house was turreted and protected by a moat. In 1627 Sir Henry Herbert, Master of the Revels, purchased it. In 1640 he was the MP for Bewdley but in 1642 he was refused permission to sit as a Member. He regained the seat after the Restoration and held it until 1673. His son Henry was returned as Member for Bewdley in 1676 and his grandson, also Henry, succeeded as Lord Herbert of Cherbury in 1708. However, he committed suicide by hanging himself in one of the turrets of Ribbesford House. His body was found by a servant who was too afraid to cut him down. In 1790 two sides of the quadrangle were demolished and the moat filled in. The house passed to the Winnington family. Major repairs and restoration were carried out in 1830.

From May 1942 to June 1944 Ribbesford House was used as a military cadet school for the Free French, the St Cyr school in exile. One student was the son of General de Gaulle. The school was commemorated in 1961 by this plaque installed by the Free French. Note the Cross of Lorraine.

Above: On the hill, centre, is Winterdyne, the seat of Sir Edward Winnington, who was Lord of the Manor. Thomas Nash in his *Collections for the History of Worcestershire*, published in 1782, recites how Sir Edward 'has lately built a new manor or mansion house, on a hill near the town, called Winterdyne, which commands a delightful view of the Severn, with its pendent rocks and woods'.

Left: Mrs Mary Gresley in 1865. She lived at Winterdyne with her husband Francis and their six children. Francis was a retired major from the East India Service.

The Music Room at Winterdyne in 1880.

Kateshill, built in the late eighteenth century by Thomas Cartwright, merchant, was originally called The Hill House. In the twentieth century it was occupied by the Whitcombe family, one of whom, Miss M. Whitcombe, recorded many of the local crafts with her camera in the 1930s. Later Dr Norman Hickin, who wrote books on the flora and fauna of the Wyre Forest, lived there. After a spell as a nursing home it has reverted to a private house.

Left: Miss Elizabeth Annie Whitcombe in around 1961, aged 103. She was the daughter of Robert Henry Whitcombe, solicitor.

Below: The Old Rectory was given to the Ecclesiastical Commissioners in 1880 by Mrs Fortescue to be used as the parsonage for the Parish of St Anne, Bewdley. The earliest reference to the building is in 1801 when it was part of the marriage settlement of Robert Pardoe the younger, when he married Elizabeth Acton. The Pardoe family continued to occupy the house until 1879 when the Reverend William Owen Parker Ford, Vicar of St Anne's, was the tenant. The vicars and rectors of the parish continued to live here until the 1980s when the property was sold back into private ownership.

The Convalescent Home in The Park, off High Street, was run by the Odd Fellows Friendly Society. They opened it in 1893 for the benefit of members residing within seventy-five miles of Birmingham. It continued to be self-supporting until the 1940s. Prior to this it had been a school for many years, taking boys from many parts of the country.

The Recreation Room at the Convalescent Home in The Park.

Above: The Old Town Hall inn at No. 19 Wyre Hill. According to a sale notice the inn had been in the ownership of one family (Cooke) for seventy-eight years. The same notice stated that it was 'an exceptional opportunity for anyone to acquire a perfectly Free Home Brewing House'. The occupant in 1891 was Joseph Oakes, a timber merchant and charcoal dealer. By 1901 he had moved out and Thomas Stone became the licensee. It eventually stopped trading as an inn in 1939 when its sales had dropped to less than a barrel of ale a week. At the time of this photograph Emmeline Walsh was the licensee.

Left: The rear of Cooke's almshouses in High Street, *c.* 1918. The eight apartments for women, who were originally chosen by the Steward of the Corporation, were completed in 1695. Each resident was to receive fifteen shillings at Christmas.

The Manor House in High Street in 1954, so called because at one time the Lord of the Manor lived there. It was a guest house in the 1930s and 1940s. During the 1950s the property was owned and managed by the Midland Adult School Union and provided accommodation for conferences and school groups of up to forty-five persons. There were two lawns on which bowls and croquet were played; table tennis and billiard tables; dart facilities in the loggia and a tennis court. The recreation room can just be seen next to the Baptist church on the extreme right. This room was converted to garages when the house was divided into apartments. They were purchased by the Baptist church in the 1980s.

This group of girls from Quarry Bank Secondary School, near Brierley Hill, was one of the many groups to use the school facilities at the Manor House in the 1950s.

Wyre Court, *c.* 1915. This property has been much altered over the years. First mention of it is in 1657 when it belonged to the Boylston family. It later passed to the Soley family, wealthy landowners. John Soley moved to Sandbourne in Wribbenhall and the property went to Thomas Cheeke, a prosperous hatter and felt-maker. In the 1850s Wilson Aylesbury Roberts owned it and after his death his natural son, Thomas Ford, took the name Roberts to continue the ownership. The property, now converted to apartments, was once used as a country club.

The interior of Beaucastle which was built in the 1870s by George Baker, a former Lord Mayor of Birmingham, in the style of John Ruskin. Baker employed the architect W. Doubleday to interpret the layout and style of the house.

Cottages on Bark Hill in 1936, before their demolition. Many of the cottages would have been occupied by craftsmen who worked in the forest and labourers at the hornworks and ropeworks.

These cottages in Lax Lane were in a bad state of repair and were going to be demolished. However, in the 1970s, after pressure from the Civic Society, they were renovated and today are very desirable homes.

Dowles Croft, on the river bank at the corner of Gas Works (now more elegantly named Greenacres) Lane decorated for King George V's Jubilee in 1935. This house no longer exists. It fell into disuse and was demolished in the 1970s. A modern building, Portlock House, now occupies the site a little further back from the river and a modern house is called Dowles Croft.

Dowles Manor from across Dowles Brook. Pevsner, in his book *Buildings of England*, describes the manor house as 'a small but exceptionally complete Elizabethan Manor House, in perfect seclusion in a dip surrounded by wood'. The manor and lordship changed hands fairly often before Samuel Skey bought it in 1783. By 1871 Edward Pease purchased it and bequeathed it to his only child, Beatrice, who became the Countess of Portsmouth. She owned many properties and land in the area but in 1902 her holdings were sold. Jannion Steele Elliott bought, restored and altered the house and later passed it to his daughter, Mrs Marjorie Sheldon. It was during her occupation that the property was destroyed by fire in January 1982.

Painsmore was once two cottages. It is thought to have been built just before Dowles Manor in the sixteenth century.

Hawkbatch Farm is just over the boundary in Shropshire. It is thought to have been built in the fifteenth century and is marked on a map of 1577. An earthwork nearby suggests that there had been clay-workings in the vicinity.

Warstone House, seen here in 1984, was originally known as Springhill House and has been the home of several carpet manufacturers. Everard Barton was perhaps the most successful. He worked with his father, John, in the business of John E. Barton & Sons in Vicar Street, Kidderminster.

Edward Richmond Nicholas, son of Reverend John Nicholas, was a solicitor. He and his wife Elianor lived at Severn House (now Mill House), Stourport Road, Wribbenhall in the 1860s and 1870s. Ellen Nicholas was their daughter.

Thomas Binyon, seen here with his wife Edith, bought Spring Grove in 1898. He was a solicitor in the London practice of Smiles & Co. and retired in his forties to live at Spring Grove. In 1914, rather than modernising Spring Grove, the family moved to Colwall, Herefordshire where they stayed until Thomas's death in 1930.

Mrs Edith Binyon is seen here outside Spring Grove, with Florence, her maid. James Butcher is the coachman. Spring Grove was built by Samuel Skey, a wealthy merchant, between 1787 and 1790. The grounds were often used for parish events. For example, in 1904 the village fête was held to raise money for an extension to the churchyard at All Saints'. A similar event in 1905 included maypole dancing and archery.

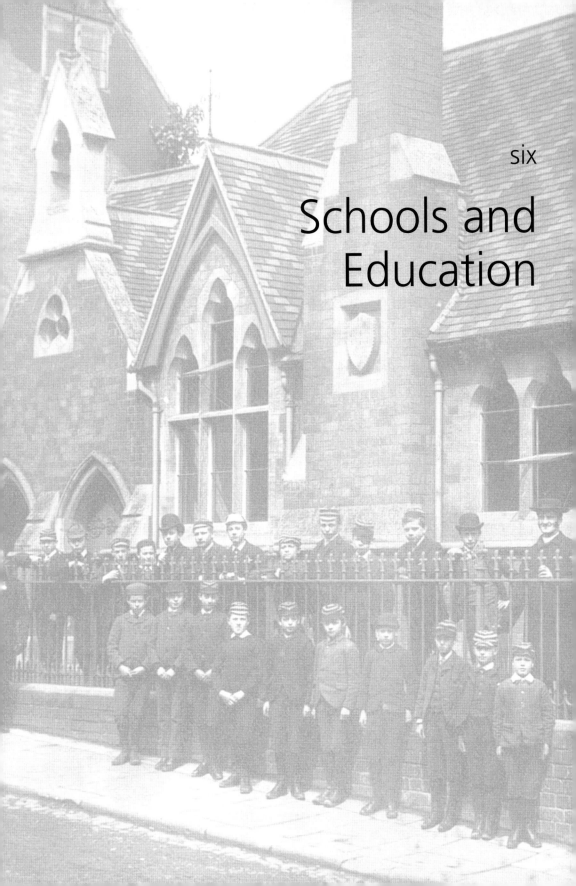

six

Schools and Education

The history of education in Bewdley begins with references to a grammar school in the sixteenth century, when a schoolroom is described as having been attached to the south side of the timber-framed chapel at the top of Load Street, though a schoolroom may have been established as early as 1483 when the stone bridge was built. The school attracted bequests of money, land and property and its affairs often appear in the Bridge and Chapel Wardens' Account Book. The first entry is in 1577 when 2s 8d was spent 'to put the scholemaster's chambers in order'.

A timber-framed house built in 1607 in The Park was on land given for the purpose of building a new grammar school. It was reported to be a very popular school in the first half of the eighteenth century when some of the pupils came as boarders from well outside Bewdley. In 1786, during the headship of the Reverend Thomas Morgan (1778-95), a tragic event took place when the smock of one of the boys caught fire. He died from his injuries.

The old grammar school was closed in 1835 through lack of pupils and the new grammar school opened in High Street in 1861. Reverend William Grist was the headmaster but was not considered to have been very competent. The Reverend John Richard Burton followed him in 1871. He was outstanding both as headmaster and in raising money for the school by his own efforts. He funded equipment for the school from scientific lectures. He wrote the first *History of Bewdley* in 1883 and a little later *The History of Kidderminster*. He received an annual salary of £80 and two-thirds of the capitation fee. However, his salary was often in arrears so it is not surprising that he accepted the position of headmaster of Kidderminster Grammar School in 1885.

In the latter half of the nineteenth century the school rarely had more than fifty boys and often many less. Most were day boys but a few stayed in the house of the headmaster. A later headmaster, Reverend J.M. Schulhof, resided in Bewdley half the week and spent the other half in Melton Mowbray where he was headmaster of another school. The grammar school closed in 1912 as a result of a school inspector's report.

During the second half of the eighteenth century and during the nineteenth century many small private day and boarding schools were established for boys and girls, including one on the top floor of Tickenhill House in the late nineteenth century. In the last quarter of the eighteenth century, appeals were made for support for charity schools that included the new Sunday schools initiated by Robert Raikes. National Schools were built in Lax Lane and in Wribbenhall by the church authorities. The Nonconformist British School in Wribbenhall was built next to the National School.

In the 1860s the Government was anxious to provide education for all and pressed those with existing premises to extend them. If this was not possible, schools governed by a Board of Trustees should be built. Negotiations were begun with the church authorities for use of the Mission Hall lately built on Wyre Hill and intended for evening services. It was eventually rented out for the use as a school and was in use until the 1950s.

Opposite above: The boys of Bewdley Grammar School pose with the Reverend J.R. Burton, *c.* 1880.

Opposite below: Another set of pupils from the grammar school, here wearing caps rather than mortar boards, are photographed in front of the school.

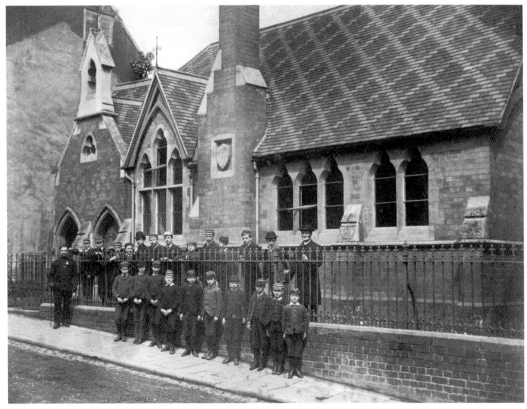

Ye friends of my heart
Ere from you I depart
This hope to my breast is most near
If again we shall meet
In this rural retreat
May we meet as we part with a Tear
May no marble bestow
The splendour of woe
Which the children of vanity rear
No fiction of fame
Shall blazon my name
All I ask all I wish is a Tear

Harriet Jones Wrought this at Mrs Almgills
School High Street Bewdley in 1826

Left: This delightful sampler gives the only evidence we have that Mrs Almgill had a school in High Street in 1826, with Harriet Jones as one of her pupils. The quality of the sampler and the words of the verse suggest that it was a small boarding school rather than a dame school. The house depicted appears to be No. 24 High Street, Bewdley, where it is known that a boarding school for girls was being run by a Mrs Susan Parsons in the 1860s and 1870s.

Below: Wyre Hill Infants' School was built in 1868 for 130 children. After the school's closure it had various uses including a printing works that moved out just before this photograph was taken in the 1960s, prior to the building's demolition. The area is now residential.

Pupils of Wyre Hill Infants' School at the beginning of the twentieth century. The mistress is possibly Miss Mann who was a teacher at the school for many years.

In the 1870s Lax Lane School was opened as a National School by the Church of England to provide education for all. It had originally been built in 1838 and was enlarged in 1912 to accommodate 340 children. This group, taken in 1888, shows quite well-dressed children but there is evidence that many children were provided with boots and stockings from the Blackford Coal, Blanket and Clothing Fund. The master was Mr William Vickrage and his wife was the mistress.

This infants' class at Lax Lane in 1920 shows pinafores still common for girls. Many have the fashionable bow of ribbon in their hair. Several of the boys are obviously wearing home-made outfits and some the hairy woollen jumpers that were so hardwearing. Many of them still wear boots. At this time the headmaster was Mr Robert Jackson and the infants' teacher Miss Kate Newell.

In 1951 Lax Lane School boys were champions of the Football League Division II. The headmaster, seen here on the extreme right of the back row, was Mr Alan Dixon.

The British School in Wribbenhall. Behind it is the National
School. In the background can be seen Christ Church shortly before
demolition in 1880.

A group of children at Wribbenhall School with their teacher Miss Daisy Wooldridge in 1914. Note the
picture of the King on the wall.

The two Wribbenhall schools, which had been combined, closed in 1978, becoming two sites again – the First School in Shaw Hedge Road and the Middle School in Stourport Road. This photograph was taken just before the move.

Girls at Wribbenhall School during an exercise class.

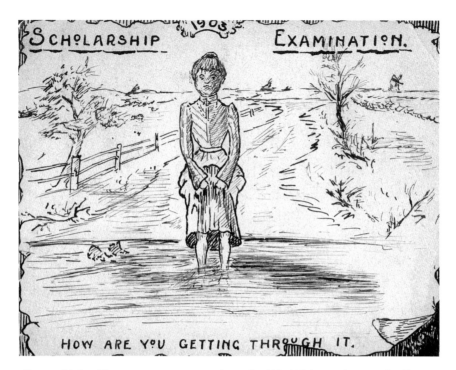

Above and below: These two cartoons were drawn by Alfred Vickrage, the son of William Vickrage, headmaster at Lax Lane School. He was listed in the 1901 census return as a lithographic artist. The drawings relate to his sister who became an elementary school teacher.

The mock timber-framed building is Bewdley Institute in Load Street, which was given to the town in 1875 by Edward Pease. In the nineteenth century strenuous efforts were made to provide adult education and a centre was set up and known as The Institute in what had been the Wheatsheaf inn in Load Street. Edward Pease donated the Institute in 1875 with the proviso that £1,000 was raised by public subscription. He later lowered this to £500. The premises opened on Monday 14 October 1878, by which time subscriptions received and a Government grant left only £200 to find. The facilities, for both men and women, consisted of a science room, two classrooms, a reading room, library, art room and bagatelle room.

The educational facilities were well used and many who attended the classes and lectures in chemistry, mathematics, drawing and many more subjects took examinations. In 1883 the library circulated 158 books and additional books were soon added. 357 volumes were borrowed during 1884 and 1885, being 'books of scientific or educational value' and 172 works of fiction. The reading room was available for anyone to look at the newspapers and journals. A membership of one penny was payable. This fee did not change for forty years!

Social activities were increased over the years and various groups – snooker and billiards, bagatelle, chess and draughts and air-gun shooting – were very successful. Each group won their league on several occasions in the nineteenth and twentieth centuries.

Until 1970 Bewdley Library was in the building at the rear of the Institute but new purpose-built premises were erected off Load Street car park. This photograph shows the Branch Librarian, Mrs Frankie Virr, helping to re-shelve all the books.

seven

Civic Occasions

These elaborate coaches and carriages are part of Bewdley's celebrations for Queen Victoria's Diamond Jubilee in 1897. Many parts of Bewdley were decorated and some streets had their own festivities.

The Coronation of George V in 1911. Welch Gate and Sandy Bank are suitably decorated for the occasion.

Mayor's Sunday, 17 November 1912. The mayor is Major R.H. Whitcombe who was also mayor the following year. To his right is Mr John Green, manager of the Midland Bank, who was mayor thirteen times. To Major Whitcombe's left is Mr Stanley Hemingway, town clerk, who was a partner of Marcy, Hemingway & Sons, solicitors.

This guard of honour is thought to be part of some celebrations for Peace Day in 1919 or 1920. The men with chains are possibly members of the Order of Buffaloes who had a Lodge in Bewdley at this time.

Guildhall,
Bewdley.

With the Compliments of the

BEWDLEY WELCOME HOME COMMITTEE.

Please accept this gift of Five Pounds from the burgesses of Bewdley as an expression of their gratitude to you for the personal service you have given to them and to your Country during the World War, September 1939, to August 1945.

Returning soldiers were rewarded for serving their country during the war.

Mayor's Sunday 1950 with Mayor William Purcell and Mayoress Mrs Elfreda Purcell. In the centre in the wig is Mr W. Bryan, town clerk. Others in the line-up include: Cllrs Raleigh Coles, Robert Jackson, Henry Neal Frost, Mrs Deenah Lawrence, William James, Frederick Bishop and Percy Palmer. Messrs Bert Perrin, Rowland Fellows, Samuel Rowe and Mrs Phyllis Phillips make up the front two rows.

Mayor William Purcell outside the Guildhall, reading the proclamation of the accession to the throne of Queen Elizabeth II in 1952.

Bewdley Town Council, 1980. From left to right, back row: Reverend Percy Lutton (chaplain), Cllr Mrs F.S. Pritchard MBE, Mr K. Smith (town clerk), Cllr R.G.B. Banks (mayor), Mr T.J. Gait (honorary treasurer), Cllr A.W.G. Wormald, Cllr D.J. Moore. Front row: Mr R.E. Wild (Sergeant at Mace), Cllr J. Hancox, Cllr Mrs L. Edginton, Cllr G.W. Haynes, Cllr A.J. Ridding, Cllr S.R. Shelter, Cllr K.J. Peers, Cllr H. Beach, Mr L. de Vroome (Sergeant at Arms).

Mr Stephen Quayle is addressing the audience in the Guildhall at a meeting to organise a petition for a bypass to help ease the traffic congestion through Bewdley. Others seated at the bench are, from left to right: Cllr Nellie Anson, -?-, Sir Tatton Brinton MP, Cllr Walter Cross (mayor), Winston O.E. Bryan (town clerk) and Cllr Joseph Garbett.

Above left: Langley Kitching was Mayor of Bewdley from 1890–1892 and 1899–1900.
Above right: Joseph Oakes was mayor from 1920–21.

Stanley Baldwin was MP for West Worcestershire and then for Bewdley. He became prime minister in 1923 and received the Freedom of the Borough of Bewdley on 8 August 1925. A true Bewdley man, he was born at Lower Park House, Lower Park. He married his wife Lucy in 1892. As Prime Minister (and good employer) he found himself dealing with the devastating General Strike in 1926. He used his experience of good working relations with his employees to good purpose in the negotiations with people and gained a reputation as a 'healer'. Ten years later he counselled King Edward VIII during the constitutional crisis that arose through the King's proposed marriage to the twice-married American Mrs Wallace Simpson. The King abdicated on 10 December 1936.

Stanley Baldwin retired to his home at Astley Hall three miles from Bewdley in May 1937. He was elevated to the House of Lords a month later and took the title Earl Baldwin of Bewdley. He died in 1947 and was succeeded by his eldest son Oliver. Stanley and Lucy Baldwin are both buried at Worcester Cathedral.

Stanley Baldwin arrives by car for the ceremony in which he will be the first Bewdley citizen to receive the Freedom of the Borough.

Leaving the car at the bridge, Baldwin, accompanied by the mayor and town clerk, walks through Load Street to the Guildhall.

This photograph shows Prime Minister Stanley Baldwin receiving the Freedom of the Borough document outside the Guildhall in Load Street. The spectators, some seated and many standing block the road.

This fine decorated casket, made by the Bromsgrove Guild, was presented to the prime minister by Mayor Alfred Maunder. It was a replica of a seventeenth-century box made in ebony, silver and leather.

A further presentation of a set of horn beakers and a spale basket (representing local trades) was made by Mr Joseph Oakes. The lady behind is Mr Oakes' second wife, Hannah.

This view shows some of the guests comfortably seated (and smartly dressed) for the occasion of the Freedom ceremony outside the Guildhall.

Above: Stanley and Lucy Baldwin outside St Anne's Cottage in Lax Lane with some of the street's residents.

Left: No present-day prime minister would be seen in an advertisement as Stanley Baldwin is here.

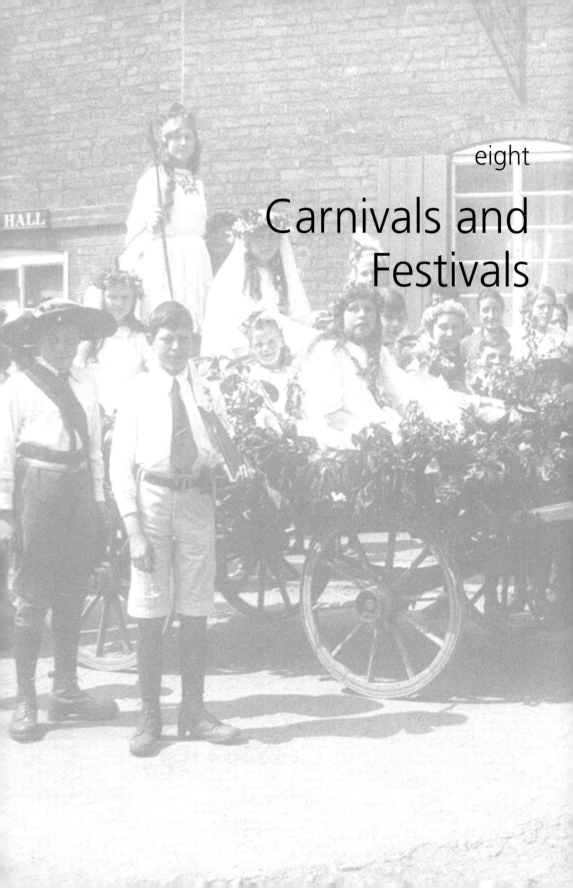

eight

Carnivals and Festivals

These celebrations are thought to be for Peace Day 1919. The Page family occupied the house on the left of The Mug House in Severn Side North. Among those posing with Mrs Page are her neighbours Mrs Norwood and Mrs Sedgley, her sons Stan and Cyril – known as Tacker – and V.G. Gale and C.B. Gale Junior.

Most inns would have put on some sort of celebration for Peace Day and this shows a gathering at the Black Boy on Wyre Hill.

In August 1926 Bewdley held a large Land and Water Carnival. As well as the procession seen here, there were decorated craft on the river, a firework display and many sideshows and events.

A carnival float pauses in Westbourne (Whispering) Street in front of Wribbenhall post office probably during the 1920s. It may have been part of the 1926 Land and Water Carnival.

Empire Day celebrations at Wribbenhall School. Empire Day was inaugurated in 1902 and was officially recognised in 1904. Celebrated annually on the anniversary of Queen Victoria's birthday, 24 May, it was intended to recognise the unity of the British Empire. In 1958 the name was changed to Commonwealth Day and the date changed to March.

Celebrations for the Coronation of King George VI in 1937, in Burlton's Terrace, off High Street. Ellen Birch and her sister Mollie Millward are standing on the step of Ellen's house. The lady with a child in her arms on the right may be Mrs Perks.

The ducking stool used to be a punishment inflicted on witches. By the 1920s it was merely a frolic at a carnival. A crowd have gathered to watch this event at the Load Street end of the bridge.

These floats travelling along Severn Side South are part of the 1947 carnival procession.

In 1851, inspired by Prince Albert, the Great Exhibition was held in the Crystal Palace. One hundred years later, during 1951, the whole of Britain held a Festival and most towns and villages held events and celebrations. Bewdley held an exhibition of items of historical interest in the Guildhall as well as a pageant and a carnival. Mrs Phyllis Phillips, centre in the hooped dress, had been mayoress to her father, Alderman Henry Frost, the previous year.

The Festival Queen's float in the 1951 Festival celebrations. Patsy Hands was the Queen and with her are, from left to right: Margaret Potter, Edna Moule, Rosemary Birch, Dorothy Edwards, -?-, Gwen Bradley.

Although the occasion is unknown – it was possibly the 1951 Festival – each of these thespians can be named. From left to right: Joe Bates, Miss Mary Moore, Charles Mackaness, Miss Tolley, Charles Albert, Miss Effie Drew.

In 1972 Princess Alexandra visited Bewdley during its quincentenary celebrations. Here she is chatting to people in Hornbeam Close, some from the sheltered housing scheme. Among those in the photograph are, next to the Princess, Mrs Wotherspoon holding Tina, Mrs Beryl Welsh and Mrs Stephens.

One of the many celebrations for the Coronation of George V. This one was on Gardner's Meadow at the bottom of Lax Lane.

These children are at a tea party in St George's Hall in celebration of the Coronation of Queen Elizabeth II in 1953.

nine

Sport and
Leisure

Excitement on Sandy Bank with motorcycles and sidecars taking part in a rally in around 1930.

The tennis club in Stourport Road opened in 1924. It was laid out on land given by Alderman Henry Frost, who can be seen in the light suit. Note the shorter skirt and simple shoes of the young lady on the right of the picture, who is clearly intending to play. By 1961 the club had a membership of eighty adults and forty juniors. The present club has seven courts – three grass and four clay.

Bewdley Musical Society.

The first Meeting for Practice will be held at the Town Hall on Monday Evening, October 3rd, at 7.30.

Locke's music in *Mackbeth*, (Price 6d.) and *An Ode to the North East wind*, by Alice Mary Smith, (Price 1s), both published by Novello, have been selected for practice and may be obtained at Messrs. F. R. & T. C. Dalley's.

JAMES L. CHESSHIRE,

Hon. Sec.

Bewdley Musical Society is thought to have had its first meeting in 1881. The Honorary Secretary sent one of these cards to each member. The date of this card is unknown.

The Garden Cinema was built in around 1920 by Mark Round on the Butt Town Meadow. This photograph of 1933 shows staff posing outside the front entrance.

Above: The Garden Cinema was demolished in 1964 and the Bridge House offices now occupy the site. In the background can be seen the former carpet factory which was later used for various businesses including the Beaulieu Chocolate Manufacturing Company.

Left: The Beaulieu Chocolate Manufacturing Company started in around 1928 and made sugar decorations for the wholesale cake market. It was owned by Charles Farmer, who can be seen here with his wife Jennifer. They lived in Springfield Villas behind the factory.

During the nineteenth and twentieth centuries, bagatelle, a game similar to billiards, was popular and these men were members of the Mug House bagatelle team. From left to right, back row: Tommy Fearnall, Sid Hunt, Harry Preece. Front row: Dick Moule, Cyril Page, Charlie Pountney, Bill Crew.

The Fossils Football Club in the 1919/20 season. It is believed that the team was the forerunner of the present Bewdley Comrades.

Among the men in this photograph of the Waggon and Horses Fishing Club are: Alf Moles, Tom Moles, Albert Garbett, Tom Darkes, George Garbett and Captain Harry Atkinson.

From the mid-nineteenth century the river has been a source of pleasure. A rowing club has existed in Bewdley from at least 1845. These young people are enjoying a rest at Blackstone before rowing back.

The Beech Cove lido, set behind the Woodman inn on the switchback road between Bewdley and Stourport, was very popular in the 1950s and 1960s.

Bewdley Cricket Club, 1963. From left to right, back row: Mark Rushton, David Flack, Mike Rawlinson, Mike Duff, Bob Duff, Geoff Rathbone, Tony Pullinger, John (Noddy) Freeman, Bob Bradley, Ted Flynn (umpire). Front row: David Woster, Ivor George, John Wadeley, Weedon Stone, Jeff Higgott, -?-. Fred Harvatt, scorer, is at the front holding the board.

Mr Jack Davies bowling the first wood on the opening of the new clubhouse at Bewdley Bowling Club in 1981. The inaugural meeting of the club was held at the George Hotel on 30 May 1902. The club met at the rear of the hotel until 1950 when it moved to its present site.

The Wyre Hill football team outside the Black Boy inn.

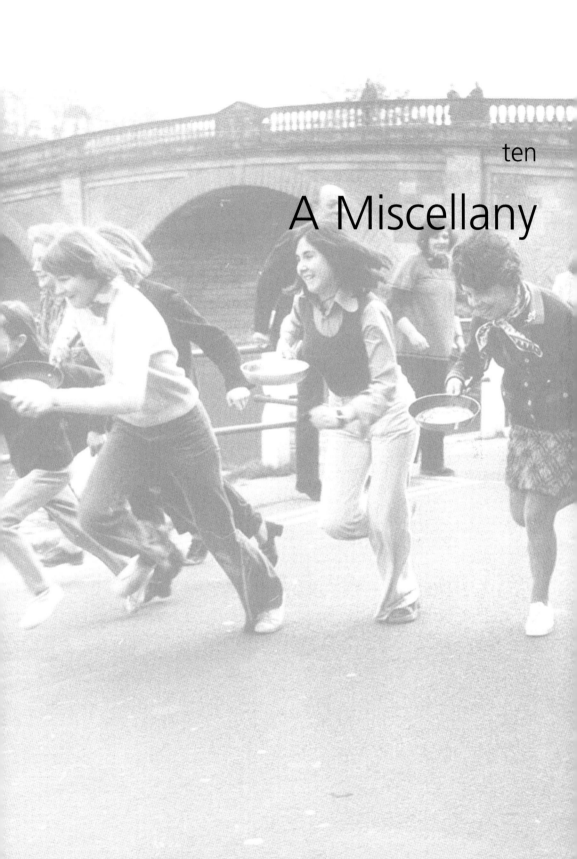

ten

A Miscellany

Bewdley and Wribbenhall from the air in the 1960s.

BEWDLEY MOTOR COMPANY, LIMITED.

CARS
FOR
HIRE

———

ALL
SUPPLIES
PETROL,
OIL, ETC.

MOTOR
CARS

MOTOR
CYCLES

———

CYCLES AND
PRAMS
REPAIRED

Motor Engineers and Garage Proprietors.

OFFICIAL REPAIRERS TO A.A., R A C A.C.U.   MOTOR HAULAGE CONTRACTORS

DAILY TRANSPORT SERVICE TO AND FROM BIRMINGHAM.

SEVERN TRANSPORT SERVICES   *LUGGAGE Collected and Delivered.*

ARTHUR EATON, MANAGING DIRECTOR.

Above and below: Presumably the bus in the photograph below has been hired from the Bewdley Motor Company Ltd. The bus is parked at the bottom of Lax Lane.

Evans Garage was at No. 7 Load Street. This photograph from around 1930 was taken before petrol pumps were installed on the frontage. The swing-arm of the pumps used to stretch across the footpath.

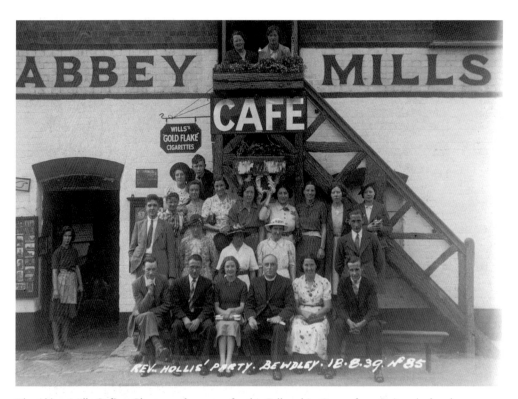

The Abbey Mills Café at Clent was the venue for this Fellowship Group from St Anne's church.

Left: These three gentlemen – Messrs Minton, Humpherson and Harcombe – are standing outside the baker's shop of Frank Heydon. They may have been judges for the window displays during the celebrations for George V's Coronation.

Below: Mayor Eric Finch is presenting service awards to Bewdley firemen Cyril Gardner, second left, and Harry Williams, left, in 1962.

This café was in Stourport Road near to Beale's Corner in the 1940s. The shop on the right was Asbury's and is now River View Stores.

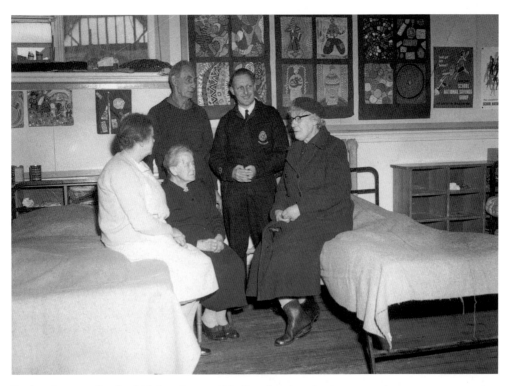

During the many floods which have happened in Bewdley there has been a need to move some people out of their homes and put them into emergency accommodation. Nurse Nellie Anson, right, who was also the mayor of Bewdley, is talking to evacuees G. and L. White and E. Bradbury. The identity of the man with the badge on his jacket is not known.

MILL AND MEADOW MONEY.

TO

THE POOR

OF THE

BOROUGH OF BEWDLEY

AND

Lordship of Ribbesford.

TAKE NOTICE

That the Charity Trustees will distribute the MILL and MEADOW MONEY, on WEDNESDAY and THURSDAY, the 10th and 11th days of February, 1858.

Persons residing in Bewdley, wishing to partake of this Charity, must give in, in writing, their Names, Places of Abode, and Number of Children, to MR. BENJAMIN JEFFERIES, at the Guildhall, Bewdley, on THURSDAY, the 4th day of February, 1858, and it is particularly requested that they attend in the following order, viz :—

1.—High Street, Lower Park, Grubber's Alley, and Park Lane.
2.—Load Street, Lax Lane, and Severn Side.
3.—Welch Gate, Brook Side, and Windbrook.
4.—Coals Quay, Doglane, Gibralter, Palmer's Building, & Venus Bank.
5.—Wyre Hill, Sandy Bank, and Barrett's Stile.
6.—Racks, Bark Hill, Lakes, Balaam's Ass, and Cockshoot.
7.—Hawthorn Bush, Tanner's Hill, Bloody Hole, and Uncles.

And persons wishing to partake of the same Charity, residing in the Lordship of Ribbesford; Park End; Lye Head; the Bliss Gate; the Forest Road, commencing at the Hawthorn Bush; and Bewdley Far Forest, to do the same on Friday the 5th day of February, 1858, at Nine o'clock in the Morning of each day, and those persons who neglect to do so, will be excluded from a share of the said distribution.

Guildhall, Bewdley, January 28th, 1858.

T. E. DALLEY, PRINTER, BEWDLEY.

Left: Mill and Meadow Money was just one of the many charities available to Bewdley residents. As well as financial support, residents could get help from the Blackford Coal, Blanket and Clothing Fund with coal, blankets and clothing, such as stockings and boots for the children. There were also several almshouses to help with accommodation.

Below: The earliest record of charitable money in Dowles is in 1571 when William Southall left rent from land in Dowles to the local parson to keep 'the yerely mindes' of himself and his wife.

A memorial of several gifts given for the use of the poor of the parish of Dowles by the persons hereunder mentioned:

By Thomas Grove of the said parish Anno Dom 1636 forty shillings.

Item By mr Walter Abbots Rector Anno Dom 1683 two pounds ten shillings.

Item By Humphry Garmston of the said parish Anno Dom 1684 ten shillings.

Item By Thomas Garmston of the said parish Anno Dom 1697 ten shillings.

the Interest of y above sd Sums is to be given to y poor yearly at Christmas.

Item By William Guy of the said parish Anno Dom 1700 ten shillings.

Item By mr Nathaniel Williams Rector ibid Anno Dom five pounds, y Interest whereof is to be laid out in buying of Books Bibles every two years. And distributed at New years Tide to such poor people of y parish of Dowles as y Rector of y sd parish for y time being shall from time to time direct and appoint.

Item By Francis Radnal December y 1703 two pounds ten shillings the interest Whereof is to be given yearly upon Candlemas day to y poor of this parish, by himself while he lives and afterward by y Rector Churchward & Overseer of y Poor.

123

Dr George Lawrence was a popular doctor in Bewdley and his wife Deenah was mayor from 1952-3. They are seen here being interviewed by Franklin Engelmann for the *Down Your Way* radio programme in 1965.

The Vickrage family, *c.* 1890. The family lived in Lower Park, firstly at No. 7 and later at No. 4. William Henry was the master of Bewdley's National School in Lax Lane and his wife Emily was the mistress. This photograph shows them with their children William, Henry, Alfred and Edith. The lady on the left is Mary Ann Vickrage, sister of William Henry, who was the housekeeper.

This troop of Cubs and Scouts were probably from the Baptist church as Miss Kathleen Quayle, who was the Cub Mistress, can be seen on the extreme right of the front row. Her brother, Stephen Quayle, was the Scout Master. The troop frequently used the nearby Wyre Forest for training.

The official opening by Major Harcourt Webb in December 1951 of the new headquarters for Scouts and Guides in Spencer Avenue, Wribbenhall.

A pancake race on Severn Side North in 1974. Although many towns and villages have held such races for many years, this was a first for Bewdley.

Before the bypass was built, Welch Gate was the main route between Birmingham and Central Wales. It was not unusual to see scenes like this one in the 1960s and 1970s. On this occasion a photographer was on hand to record the event.

The pathway along the riverbank, having crossed in front of the hermitage, passes behind Blackstone Rock on its way to Stourport.

A postcard sent from Bewdley, showing views of the town.

Other local titles published by Tempus

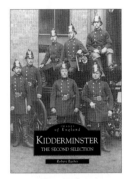

Kidderminster: The Second Selection
ROBERT BARBER

This intriguing compilation of photographs provides a delightful insight into this Worcestershire town. The history of the town's great companies, both past and present, are explored including Brinton's Carpet Company, T. & A. Naylor, The Castle Motor Company, and the Sugar Factory which recently closed after seventy-seven years of production.

0-7524-2619-2

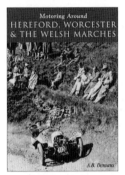

Motoring Around Hereford, Worcester & The Welsh Marches
A.B. DEMAUS

This richly illustrated volume on motoring in Hereford, Worcester and the Welsh Marches shows the many uses that wheeled transport has been put to. There are bicycles, cars of all shapes, sizes and ages, lorries, steam traction engines as well as views of motor sport in the area. Covered in detail are local manufacturers such as Morgan, now one of the largest independent motor manufacturers left in Britain.

0-7524-2361-4

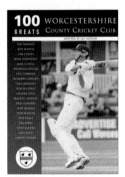

Worcestershire CCC: 100 Greats
LES HATTON

Worcestershire celebrated 100 years of first-class cricket in 1999, but after the struggling days of the 1920s it is perhaps lucky that the club still survives at all. This volume celebrates Worcestershire's 100 greatest players and is compiled by Les Hatton, the club's statistician and editor of the ACS Second Eleven Annual, with a foreword by Tim Curtis.

0-7524-2194-8

Bromsgrove
MARGARET COOPER

The old market town of Bromsgrove, midway between Worcester and Birmingham, has long been a focal point for the surrounding villages and hamlets. This fascinating collection of over 200 photographs, which comes from the private collections of local residents, shows how Bromsgrove has changed over the last century, and how the area has progressed while maintaining a profound respect for its past.

0-7524-1146-2

If you are interested in purchasing other books published by Tempus, or in case you have difficulty finding any Tempus books in your local bookshop, you can also place orders directly through our website

www.tempus-publishing.com